The Po...
Activity Bo...

Calling all Moshling hunters! Greetings, Buster Bumblechops, super Moshling expert, here. Now, although I am fangtastic at catching these tricky little critters, I might just need your help today, because a few of them are proving more than a bit difficult to catch. Keep your eyes peeled (not literally!) in the pages of this book, for Penny, Gabby and HipHop, they're teeny-weeny masters of hide-and-seek. Happy hunting!

Can you also spy the Eye Lighthouse somewhere in this book?

The Port Quiz

There is always something going on in Monstro City's bustling Port. Monsters come from all over town to shop, stroll, swim, fish and boat. Not a lot goes unobserved, but how observant are you?

1. Who docks the *Cloudy Cloth Clipper* in The Port when he returns from his adventures?

2. Which all-seeing building stands at the edge of The Port?

3. What two kinds of seeds can you buy at Super Seeds that you can't buy anywhere else?

4. What grows on trees in The Port?

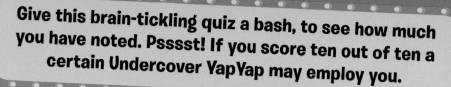

Give this brain-tickling quiz a bash, to see how much you have noted. Psssst! If you score ten out of ten a certain Undercover YapYap may employ you.

5. What three items are hanging on the back wall in Babs' Boutique?

6. Name the local jazz musician who is always fishing in The Port? What does he always catch?

7. What item sits in a nest on the back shelves in Paws 'n' Claws?

8. Which island can you take a ferry to from The Port?

9. Which two very large sea creatures can often be seen swimming in the waters around The Port?

10. Who floats in his purple spotted rubber ring in the waters of The Port?

Write your answers here.

1.

2.

3.

4.

5.

6

7.

8.

9.

10.

BABS' BOUTIQUE
Hairdos

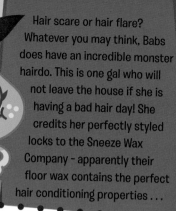

Hair scare or hair flare? Whatever you may think, Babs does have an incredible monster hairdo. This is one gal who will not leave the house if she is having a bad hair day! She credits her perfectly styled locks to the Sneeze Wax Company - apparently their floor wax contains the perfect hair conditioning properties . . .

Style up Babs with some new crazy hairdos, then pop down the shops to get yourself some Sneeze Wax. Hairtastic!

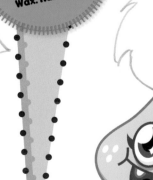

4

Wi----le Wo----l------

Roland has been on the bottle again! He thinks it will make him grow, but after the tenth bottle of this wonder wobble, his head and belly are so sloshy with all the bubbles, he can't even stand up to see how tall he is. Can you count how many bottles of Wobble-ade Roland has drunk today? Which balls of badness have come to join Roland for some bubble fun?

Tamara Tesla's Tricky Tests

Flex your antennae and boot up your brain. Monstro City's brainy scientist, Tamara Tesla, has spent another night in her lab inventing more tricky tests to try out on her monster mates. Take a deep breath, grab a pen, and pit your wits against the brainiest braniac you'll ever meet.

1 $0 \times 12 =$

2 $32 \div 8 =$

3 $333 - 222 =$

4 $2 + 4 + 6 + 8 =$

5 $7 \times 6 =$

6 $100 \div 4 =$

7 $(27 - 5) \div 2 =$

8 $1037 + 663 =$

9 You have fifty Rox. You want to give your five best monster mates an equal amount of Rox each. How many Rox will your five friends each get?

10 A new Stone Fireplace for your house will cost you ninety-nine Rox. You have 256 Rox. How many Rox will you have left to buy something else for your house?

11 If you add Ecto (#60) and Doris (#40) together, what do you get?

12 If you take Fifi (#07) away from Big Bad Bill (#89), what do you get?

Observatory Observations

Tamara Tesla has invited you to the Observatory to take a look through the Mubble Telescope. Fangtastic! Look at these four spectacular views. **Now turn the page and test your monster memory, to see how observant you really are.**

Observatory Observations

Take Tamara's test to see if your powers of observation match those of the mistress of Observatory Observing (try saying that after a few Toad Sodas!). Eyes peeled, pen at the ready, three, two, one . . .

1 What kind of house can you see in the first view through the telescope?

2 What two colours is the house?

3 Which Moshling appears on the balcony of the house?

4 What kind of monster is running away from the house?

5 How many striped umbrellas are there on Music Island beach?

6 Name three types of instrument that you can see on Music Island.

7 How many yellow towers are there on the Gift Factory?

8 How many mushrooms are growing on the tree in the garden?

9 What colour are the Scarecrow's two button eyes?

10 Who is the orange and yellow bird that sits in the tree in the garden and what does he do?

PAWS'N'CLAWS
Mystery Boxes

Looking for something monstrously unusual or need some Moshling memorabilia? Then flip-flap-flop down to Gilbert Finnster's shop. The fishy Finnster has got a sale on Mystery Boxes today. Take a peek, you never know what you might find!

Read the clues and then unwrap to reveal . . .

A

Roland's favourite fizzy, wibbly, wobbly drink.

B

This little Beastie gets terrible flaming hiccups - stand back!

C

Super sticky with just a hint of icky, but I won't make you sicky!

D

You can sit on me and I'm just gripping!

E

This sparkly Secret Moshling needs to be handled with care!

9

Finntastic Finnster Codebreaker

Gilbert Finnster's love of Moshlings began when he was just a tadpole. He has made it his quest ever since to monitor Moshling activity in his garden, and provide Moshling codes to his friends. His zoo is pretty full, but he is always on the look out for new and rare little critters.

Crack the Finntastic Moshling code and find out what his latest secret, flashy (hint hint!) Moshling quest is! Flap those fins my fishy friends!

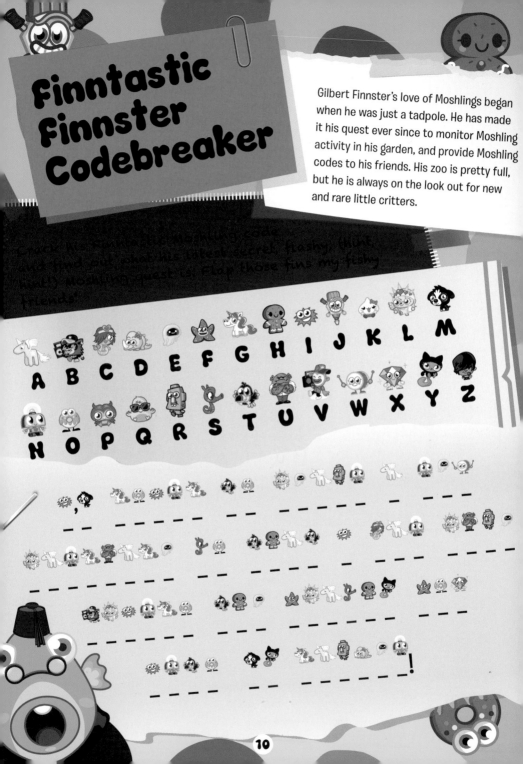

Stacey Grace's
Shoelace Scramble

Shambling shoelaces! Poor scatty Stacey Grace just can't get the hang of those snake-like shoe strings. She's always tripping over her toes as she makes her way through The Port to Miss Jingle's School for Girls. Help Stacey untangle the letters she picks up on the way to school, to reveal the purring friend she is meeting on The Port bridge.

__ __ __ __ __ __ __ __ __ __ __

SUPER SEEDS Sudoku

Three monster flowers in a row,
Chosen from a selection of super seeds to grow.
Visit my monster garden patch,
To see which little Moshlings I can catch!

....

Sow your super seeds in the garden grid below.
Remember, each of the six seed types must only
appear once on each horizontal and vertical line,
and each 6 x 6 box.

Colorama
Moshlings

Mish, mash, Moshling! Gilbert Finnster thinks he has discovered a new category of Moshlings that love hanging around the waters of The Port. While he is cracking the codes for these new little critters, grab a pen and draw the four new Moshling pets here. What are their names, and what do you think this new category of cute critters should be called?

Where are the Fishies?

Fill in the number of times you can find each Moshling in the circles below.

All about Pretty Poppet!

Awww, shucks! You can't help but stare at these big-eyed, cuddly, little Moshis. Nothing makes them happier than getting down on the dance floor - those titchy paws and stylish boots were made for boogying! But don't annoy these precious Poppets, otherwise your ears will be ringing - they can scream, and I mean S C R E A M! Owwww!

Name:

....

My Owner Name:

....

Owner's Age:

....

My Owner's Language:

....

I'm Feeling:

....

My Owner Is Feeling:

....

My Owner's Favourite Activity:

....

My Favourite Moshling:

....

My Owner's Favourite Moshling:

....

Colour your own huggalicious friend and fill in all the details on the Moshi profile card.

Answers

Page 1
Penny is hidden on page 5; HipHop is hidden on page 6; Gabby is hidden on page 8; the Eye Lighthouse is hidden on page 11.

Pages 2-3
The Port Quiz
1. Cap'n Buck.
2. The Observatory.
3. Crazy Daisy and Snap Apple.
4. Rox.
5. Two maps and a compass.
6. Beau Squiddly and he always catches boots.
7. A large egg.
8. Gift Island
9. Gail and Octo.
10. Lenny Lard.

Page 5
Wibble Wobble-ade
There are 96 bottles of Wobble Ade.
ROCKO, FREAKFACE, and FABIO have come to have some bubble fun with Roland.

Page 6
Tamara Tesla's Tricky Tests
1. 0 x 12 = 0
2. 32 ÷ 8 = 4
3. 333 - 222 = 111
4. 2 + 4 + 6 + 8 = 20
5. 7 x 6 = 42
6. 100 ÷ 4 = 25
7. (27 - 5) ÷ 2 = 11
8. 1037 + 663 = 1700
9. 10 Rox each.
10. 157 Rox
11. 100
12. 82

Page 8
Observatory Observations
1. A Haunted House.
2. Purple and green.
3. Liberty.
4. A Furi.
5. There are three striped umbrellas on the beach.
6. A guitar-shaped pool; a piano keyboard bridge; three drum-shaped hills.
7. There are three yellow towers on the Gift Factory.
8. Two.
9. Scarecrow's eyes are yellow and pink.
10. The bird is Cluekoo. He keeps an eye on your garden when you are not there and will tell you if any little Moshlings have been by for a nibble of your flowers.

Page 9
Paws'n'Claws Mystery Boxes
A. A bottle of Wobble Ade
B. Burnie
C. Barfmallows
D. Arm Chair
E. Roxy

Page 10
Finntastic Finnster Codebreaker
I'M GOING TO LEARN A NEW LANGUAGE SO THAT I CAN LURE BLINGO THE FLASHY FOX INTO MY GARDEN!

Page 11
Stacey Grace's Shoelace Maze
Stacey Grace is meeting Mr. Meowford.

Page 12
Super Seeds Sudoku

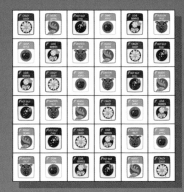

Page 14
Where are the Fishies?

1 Blurp
2 Stanleys
2 Fumbles
3 Calis